We Must Protect
Old-Growth Forests

Written by Jenny Feely

Flying Start
to Literacy®

T0363485

Contents

Introduction

An old-growth forest is a forest that has been growing in the same place for thousands of years. Many different types of trees and plants grow in old-growth forests. These plants are different sizes and ages. In old-growth forests, a lot of the trees are very, very old and they can be enormous.

These forests have been growing for thousands of years without people cutting down the trees or building roads, houses and other buildings in them.

At one time, many of the forests on the Earth were old-growth forests, but now in a lot of places in the world, fewer than 10 percent of old-growth forests are left. This book argues why these last, precious old-growth forests should be protected.

Did you know?

There are old-growth forests in countries all over the world including Australia, the USA, Brazil and Russia.

Gone forever

Old-growth forests cannot be replaced. If they are cut down, they will be gone forever. This must not be allowed to happen because old-growth forests are important places for people, plants and animals.

If you have never been to an old-growth forest you may not know what it is like. Imagine standing next to a tree that is so tall that it seems to touch the sky, with a trunk so wide that you can't see around it; a tree that has been growing in the same place for thousands of years.

Old-growth forests are the only places where you can see such amazing trees.

But sadly, every day in old-growth forests these wonderful big, old trees are being cut down. Sometimes they are cut down because their huge trunks are made of very valuable wood. Sometimes they are cut down so that the land they grow on can be used for farming. This destruction is a terrible thing. These amazing forests must be protected.

Usually all of the trees in an area are cut down, completely destroying a section of the old-growth forest. Trees in old-growth forests can't be replaced. Planting young trees of the same kind completely changes the forest. If this is done, the forest is no longer an old-growth forest.

Did you know?

It is estimated that an area of old-growth forest the same size as a football field is cut down every second.

All that is left of this tree
is this big stump.

The trees that are cut down
are stripped of their branches.

Giants of the land

The ancient trees that can only be found in old-growth forests are the biggest and oldest living things on the Earth. They are often more than 500 years old and more than 90 metres tall. They can have trunks that are more than six metres wide.

Some trees in old-growth forests are so big that they have been given names. The General Sherman tree in California, USA, is a giant sequoia tree that is 2200 years old. This tree is thought to be the biggest tree in the world and every year it grows even bigger.

Compare the size of the people at the base of General Sherman to the tree.

General Sherman tree
- As heavy as 10 blue whales
- As tall as a 27-storey building

If old-growth forests are cut down, trees like General Sherman will be gone forever. It is because they are so big that the timber industry wants to cut these trees down. Their wood is worth a lot of money because it can be used to make furniture. But no amount of money is enough to make up for the loss of these amazing trees, and no piece of furniture is as beautiful as a giant tree growing in a healthy old-growth forest.

In this forest, all the trees in one area are being cut down.

Did you know?

In the northwest of the USA, up to 90 percent of the old-growth forests have been cut down.

Healthy forests, healthy planet

Old-growth forests help to keep people healthy. They help to clean the air we breathe and the water we drink.

Clean air

The air that we breathe has a gas in it called carbon dioxide. Trees absorb carbon dioxide from the air and use it to grow their trunks, roots and leaves. The carbon dioxide is then kept in the trees.

The older the tree is, the more carbon dioxide it has stored in it. When trees in old-growth forests are cut down, the carbon dioxide stored in them is released into the air, and this is very bad for the environment. Too much carbon dioxide in the air can be harmful to our environment.

Did you know?

When a giant tree in an old-growth forest is cut down, the leaves and small branches from the tree are burned. This releases carbon dioxide into the air.

Clean water

Old-growth forests grow in places where there is a lot of rainfall. This is because trees need a lot of water to grow. As the rain falls on the trees, it trickles through the leaves and branches and onto the ground, then it flows toward streams and rivers.

The big roots of the huge trees hold the soil tightly and stop it from being washed into the streams and rivers with the water. This process cleans the water. The pure water flows out of forests and is collected and stored so it can be used as drinking water by people in cities and towns.

When old-growth forests are cut down, there is nothing to stop the rain from washing the soil into rivers and lakes. Without the trees to hold the soil, there are landslides and mudslides. Also, once this rich, healthy soil is washed away, nothing will grow where the forest once stood.

This tree helps to clean the water in the river.

4

Protect the forests, protect the animals

There are thousands of different plants and animals that live in old-growth forests. Most of the animals find their food there. Many need the shelter of the forest to raise their young. Many animals cannot survive anywhere else.

This bird has made its nest in a hollow that has formed in an old tree.

Trees in old-growth forests are all different ages. Some are seedlings just beginning to grow, while others are huge, fully grown trees. In a healthy old-growth forest, there are also a lot of dead trees called stags. Some of these are still standing, while others have fallen to the ground.

All of these trees are important for the health of the plants and animals that live in the old-growth forest. These plants and animals depend on different types of trees as well as trees that are different ages.

A stag lies on the forest floor among trees of all different ages.

an orangutan in the wild

Did you know?

Many endangered animals live in old-growth forests, such as the Northern Spotted Owl in the USA and Canada. There are fewer than 5000 of these owls in the wild.

Older trees and stags are very important to many animals. As the trees get older, hollows form in their trunks and branches. Many animals use these hollows for shelter. Some raise their babies in the tree hollows. When these old trees are cut down, the animals don't have anywhere to live. Newly planted trees take many years to form hollows.

Some animals such as orangutans and giant pandas are now endangered because the old-growth forests that they need for food and shelter have been cut down. By protecting these old-growth forests, these animals are also protected.

Chapter 5

Act now to save the forest

There are different ways that we can help to protect old-growth forests.

Often governments make laws that help to protect old-growth forests. But sometimes there are not enough laws, or there are still ways for companies to log old-growth forests without breaking the law. More laws and stricter laws are needed to prevent the destruction of old-growth forests. You can help by writing to your state government to say how you feel about this issue.

These people want to stop timber companies from cutting down old-growth forests.

You can also help to protect old-growth forests by refusing to buy products that have been made using trees from old-growth forests. These include products made from old-growth wood, such as some furniture.

Visiting your nearest old-growth forest is another way to help. If there are a lot of tourists going to visit an old-growth forest, people are less likely to destroy it.

People can walk through the treetops of this old-growth forest.

One town where this has happened is in Tasmania, Australia. The town of Geeveston used to make money from cutting down trees, but now it makes money from people coming to visit the old-growth forest nearby. The people of Geeveston built the tallest, longest airwalk in the southern hemisphere. The airwalk is like a bridge that winds through the treetops. Thousands of tourists visit the town every year to see this old-growth forest.

Conclusion

"I speak for the trees,
for the trees have no tongues."

The Lorax, Dr Seuss, 1971

If we don't speak for the trees and protect the wonderful old-growth forests they grow in, they will be gone forever. It is up to us to look after the trees and protect them so that they can continue to do their job and be enjoyed by people now and in the future.

Index

A note from the author

My favourite place to go on holiday is the mountains, where I love to walk among the huge old trees that grow there. Gazing up at a tree that began life before my great-great-grandfather was born fills me with wonder.

When I was looking for a topic that explored the environment, forests came quickly to mind. As I researched this topic I discovered that in many places around the world, trees that are hundreds of years old are being cut down. I think this is terrible, so I wrote this book as an argument to persuade people to look after old-growth forests.